GLOS[illegible]

MW01399353

A Comprehensive Guide On How To Care And Breed Glossy Snake.

Christopher Liam

Table of Contents

CHAPTER ONE

GLOSSY SNAKE

What is Glossy Snake? The Arizona may be a monotypic genus with its species being glossy snake. The prototype is actually two examples accumulated at the 'Within Arkansas and Cimarron' River, Oklahoma, and lower Rio Grande, Texas.

SUBSPECIES

1) Desert Arizona elegans. Arizona elegans eburnata. This subspecies is found within the west and southwest of Arizona. A pale milk brown shade with light olive-brown blemishes on the rear and surfaces and lightweight, bare underneath. Frequently more faded and features a smaller tail concerning body measurement than the opposite subspecies.

2) Arizona glossy snake: Arizona elegans noctivaga. This subspecies is observed across most utmost of south-central Arizona. It's a smaller tailpiece relevant to border extent than

the Painted Desert Arizona elegans.

3) Painted Desert Arizona elegans:

Arizona elegans philipi. This subspecies is discovered within the elevated area of north-east of Arizona and therefore the distant southeastern fringe of the land. Just like the western Glossy Snakes, it's a profound number of 27 flake series, but just like the eastern Glossy Snakes, it's a more extended tailpiece concerning its body diameter.

4) California Desert Arizona elegans.

A medium-sized husky serpent

with sleek, glossy scales, pale or washed-out features, and a little tail. Frequently duller than other California Arizona elegans subspecies – a brown or vivid

brown mineral with chocolate sp -ots with dull sides on the rear and surfaces and lightweight, spotless underneath.

5) Mohave Western Arizona elegans.

This subspecies transpires from the east into southwestern Nevada, and Inyo County south through most of the Mojave . A medium-sized muscular snake with glossy scales, smooth, a faded or bleached-out appearance (a pale tan, grayish, milk, or rosy earth pigment with tan-brown or gray blemishes on rear and surfaces with black frames and a pale, bare underside), and little tail.

6) Texas Arizona elegans. It is found within the Chihuahuan Desert region of northern Mexico and therefore the southwestern U.S . Its scope projects that of other Arizona elegans subspecies, and crossbreeding is feasible. The Texas Arizona elegans is usually a dark brown, with deeper copper-colored blemishes

below the expanse of the rear. 7) Kansas Arizona elegans. It has a pale brown frame with deep spots working down the core of its back. Smaller blemishes are seen along its surfaces. The abdomen is dull and light-shaded, and it's one anal plate.

8) Peninsula Arizona elegans. It transpires on the Pacific appraised of the southern portion of the Lower California point, besides for its entire southernmost range. This species is seen as distant north as El Parador in Baja, California,

to 12.4 miles north of the town of los angeles Paz, Lower California Sur.

CHAPTER TWO

APPEARANCE AND SIZE

Glossy snake, alternatively popular like the faded snake, may be a name applied to define a gaggle of serpent observed frequently in some portions of Mexico and therefore the southwestern area of the U.S. Found mostly in Arizona, alongside another subspecies, is that the elegans, which is that the most notable of the snake species. The snake doesn't deliver poison. Its sleek coverings present it a glossy appearance. The Arizona elegans holds a body-shade which varies between tan to brown, modeled with dull blemishes; with milk or whitish sew its abdomen. The snake's complexion becomes bleached or softened when lounging beneath the sun. Though having substantial connections with some species of vermin, like the gopher snake, the glossy snake's crescent pupil gives it simple to be classified. Most of their subspecies are below 100 cm in expansion, but he Arizona elegans can stretch to a supreme entire body portion of

177.8 cm. Males are smaller than females and serve 13-17% of their bodies are tail lengths. Female TL can designate 12-15% of their bodies. Offspring standard 24.8 cm in total linear unit. Hinging on the subspecies, the size series at the mid-frame span within 25-35. The posterior flakes during this species are level. Two of the more prominent features of this species are the acute nozzle and therefore the countersunk inferior mandible. Added, less visible aspect is that the generally egg-shaped pupil.

GEOGRAPHICAL RANGE

Glossy snakes are located within the Mexico and U.S . In the U.S., their range incorporates southern Nevada, southern and central California, eastern and southern Colorado, southern Utah, southern Nebraska, New Mexico, all of Arizona, Kansas, Texas, and Oklahoma. In Mexico, they're discovered continuing south within the central region of the country to Aguascalientes and Tamaulipas, also as across the Baja Penninsula to merely northward of Los Angeles Paz.

This snake is discovered beyond the western and southwestern wildernesses, the northeastern plains, and therefore the southeastern canyons in Arizona. It transpires at altitudes varying from bordering water level along the Colorado River to just about 6,000′.

HABITAT

Glossy snakes reside semi-arid fields, dry, granular wastelands and scrub, and rocky canyons, favoring open fields and loamy or sandy soil. Most are seen slightly above water level; they will be seen from beneath sea level to just about 2,220 meters beyond water level.

COMMON BEHAVIOR

Glossy snakes aren't notable for engaging in social activities aside from the coupling or any sort of authorities. There are not any distinct exemplars of concurrence or population dynamics in tropical-temperate snakes. Glossy snakes aren't known to guard areas nor formulate rankings but popular to be tender and delicate.

Glossy snakes drive managing a winding movement referred to as a parallel wave. they're skilled miners and sometimes utilize fissures or mice tunnels as refuges throughout the day. They gloomy and night-loving and are frequently most efficient within April and September (this can alter somewhat hinging on range and altitude).

Glossy Snakes unusually are energetic during the daytime. The moderately steeply egg-shaped pupil that this serpent s has is an adjustment for night perception, simultaneously with its retina, which holds both cones and rods. Annually, Arizona elegans is active in New Mexico, Arizona, and Southern California activity has been witnessed from late February or early March until November; and in Colorado from May to October. Throughout winter, the Arizona elegans sleeps hidden in an animal tunnel or immersed into the soil beneath the freeze line. Most of the Glossy Snake's outside movement takes place within May, June, and July. If hidden, the Arizona elegans may seldom rise up to the surface to relish in hot, bright, winter holidays

COMMUNICATION AND PERCEPTION

Glossy snakes apply pheromones and fragrance imprinting during breeding. Letting possible partners discover her, a female gives a trace of pheromones scoring the territory. Males recognize this smell within their vomeronasal gland. By actuating over females, males launch relations.

Both males and females snap their tongues bent take the air, delivering biochemical smells toward the mouth, pushing the air upon the roof of their jaws and beneath their nostrils where the vomeronasal gland is placed. Dwelling subterrene throughout the day, and have comparatively small eyes; glossy snakes are excavating creatures. These eyes aren't the principal sensible course adopted for identifying the victim; hence, they're primarily employed to differentiate a variation between light and dark.

CHAPTER THREE

INFORMATIONS ABOUT GLOSSY SNAKE

Glossy snakes are carnivorous. Including western whiptails, zebra-tailed lizards, blemished leaf-nosed serpents, desert iguanas, coast horned lizards, greater short-horned lizards, desert night lizards, desert spiny lizards, and general side-blotched lizards, nearly some of their nutrition is comprised of various reptiles.

The remnant of their intake consists of

small animals like Ord's kangaroo rats, long-tailed pocket rodents, Merriam's kangaroo rats, Salinas pocket mice, eastern moles, and little fowl. Unconventional trapping procedures may live for seizing several prey varieties. Portions of prey species inside nutrition are instantly related to the quantity and mass of a given serpent: Glossy snakes that devour more raptors are more comprehensive than people who absorb more animals, which are more considerable than people who essentially eat small reptiles.

THINGS YOU NEED TO KNOW ABOUT GLOSSY SNAKE

Reproduction & Life Cycle:

No particular information remains concerning the copulating method of glossy snakes. Usually, she exudes hormones which will be recognized by males through their vomeronasal glands when a female serpent is willing to possess her eggs propagated. Males grasp this smell and pursue the feminine by slithering over her. Enabling physical implantation through the cloaca, she mounts her tail if she affirms. Males and females possess numerous partners. Glossy snakes are oviparous and reproduce within the springtime and summertime after revival from slumber. Females generally produce clasps of eggs that bear from late August to mid-September, in early July. The broodings are nearly 25 cm long at parturition. There's proof that a female will produce eggs solely every distinct year, and females provide hardly one grasp of eggs per annum. Female glossy snakes are witnessed defending their baby for several days following delivery. There's no familial venture from males.

Development:

With temperature like the principal inducer, even within the inadequacy of photoperiods, spermatogenesis is periodically and transpires in late summertime. Vitellogenesis works within the spring, and ovulation can transpire in June. Fetuses emerge inside eggs yielded clandestinely by females. Overall, serpents that bear from eggs possess an egg fang on their uppermost lip, which they apply to grind their system out of the egg crust. Member is defined by the egg instead of the sperm, and this is often the ZW system; males are ZZ while females are ZW. Offsprings are developed and self-sufficient; they are doing not experience modification. Serpents spread throughout their existences, typically in 1-9 years, although pace decreases extremely once development is attained.

Lifespan/Longevity:

No information applies concerning the time on earth of

glossy snakes; commonly addressing, snakes remain from 4-25 years within the native.

HOW TO BREED GLOSSY SNAKE

Snake breeding alters a touch within different species, but there are some fundamental forethoughts you want to get a glimpse at to form certain your snake is fit, both before and subsequent . reproducing.

PLANNING TO BREED

To equip your pet snake for breeding, do convince to provide it the precise measure of energy. Serpents are usually satisfied with the heat of 85° to 100° Fahrenheit. Furthermore, plan to abstain from touching your snake following filling it, as this might induce them to disgorge their snacks. Establish A Slumber Chamber:

Hibernation is often a fundamental factor for favorably reproducing snakes, hinging on the prototype you possess. You'll have to give your snake with the aloofness of a hibernation room. To make one, get a case merely a couple of bits tinier than your snake's enclosure. Load it with five to 10 measures of corncob bedding, or different quite comparable substrates. Your serpent will dwell during this. You'll likewise desire to urge certain you sustain a continuing temperature of 55° to 60° Fahrenheit during this room.

Hibernation:

To equip your snake for slumber, assess your female's well-being with the guidance of your pet's doctor. You want to provide your pet lukewarm showers every day the week before snoozing. This may further eliminate rubbish from your pet's body. It's an excellent approach to scale back the warmth gradually in your snake's enclosure. Reduce the warmth of the bathwater several ranges every day until it's the equivalent temperature like the relaxation burrow. Settle your serpent to the hibernation container and obtain bound to supplement a dish of water also. Allow your serpent there for a couple of weeks and replace the water as needed.

Start to boost the temperature of the hibernation container subsequent weeks until it approaches the quality heat of the breathing regions. After this, you'll reinstate the serpent to its conventional enclosure.

Acquaint The Two:

You now require to precede your female to the male’s enclosure. By understanding her body expression, reflect her enthusiasm to breed. She is about if she sprawls down and seems loafed near the male. Reestablish your pet for several days in sequence until the feminine seems like she has forgotten interest within the male. She is going to be giving eggs at this era. Following this, all you want to do is to stay for her to supply eggs or delivery, energetic juniors. The pregnancy phase is typically 28 to 45 days.

CHAPTER FOUR

CARE OF THE GLOSSY SNAKE

A pet vermin requires an area and a burrow-home within the cage. Select one for your glossy pet, and then choose out substrate elements. Glossy snakes flourish during a manageable, low-maintenance cage. A grown-up are often accommodated during
a container covering 72 cms long, 30 cms broad and 30 cms high, with a decent shield cover. More comprehensive rooms are

often employed, also as more miniature enclosures for tinier serpents.

1. Substrate:

All snakes need a hidey-home. These are the things that fill the ground of the container. There are dirt and gravels and compost which
may approximately mimic the snake's fundamental territory. This could be a hollow composed of stone or a neighborhood of a neat board that the serpent matches beneath. It requires a

spot where it appears secure to sleep and relax. These are excellent.

Numerous sheets of paper can likewise take the work accomplished. It’s accessible to possess the newsprint neat and dusty,

and it's considerably cheaper.

Though the nearer to a fundamental

territory you'll accomplish, the more robust your serpent are going to be in an extended period.

Bedding is often copper wood, case or enclosure matting. Set a warming mat below one fringe of the container to put in some extent of nearly 32 degrees Celcius. The rest of the space can hold from 24 to 27 degrees.

2. Lighting & Temperature:

Some vermins will necessitate an ultraviolet-Beam light. Some won't. Some will go onward modestly with portion an hour of utmost light a day. Examine the features of your serpent's requirements. All vermins will demand a lounging light. Place it above a specific basking stone or twig.

You'll require a spread of thermostats and hygrometers (tools that regulate moisture): some for the basement and a few for the surfaces of the vivarium. Never, ever consider the thermostats. All serpents must likewise possess some under-container warming. You demand to take care here: You don't merely attach a warming mat beneath the container, set it on, and disrespect it. It necessitates being scanty enough to supply energy to the sole section of the basement, following section of the burrow-home. The aim is to present what's named a heat inclination. That suggests that one segment of the bottom beneath a hidey-home must be a specific heat. Moisture alters, solely for the foremost section; it can vary from nothing to 50 percent for this wilderness serpent. Put a water basin at the cold edge, merely large enough for the vermin to sip from. Burrows are important, as these pets consume most of its day buried beneath stones and such within the native. Various tunnels are suggested.

Illumination isn't essential.

3. Feeding:

All vermins are carnivores. They consume the whole meat, with all the bones and entrails still inside. Several species of pet serpents devour rodents and muskrats. Some consume amphibians, other lizards. The littlest ones might exist on big pests.

Luckily, several pet snakes will take stagnant prey. If yours does, think to possess a definite tiny fridge for what's cautiously described as prey objects. Lifeless rodents and mice of diverse terms are often obtained in chilled packs through pet grocery shops and instantly from somebody who reproduces diner mice.

It's best suited to possess your snake's feast independently from your meals, for wellness purposes. She might hardly swallow one, or she might swallow several at one feed, hinging on the condition of the snake. In any circumstance, you'll require to possess a share dozen available. Attempt commencing with victim pieces that are nearly the equivalent volume round the core as your pet is.

Attempt shaking the snack a touch, to urge it to maneuver if your pet won't taste lifeless victim parts. Furthermore, I strive to put a neighborhood of fabric across the container as an isolation screen. Seldom will one or both of those give the know-how.

You might require to satisfy your serpent real victim if that displeases. This is often more complex, and not for the stupor soul.

Merely like it does for other creatures, freshwater is important for serpents. Fresh and replenish her water dish at abrupt twice every week.

4. Grooming:

Grooming is most crucial when your pet discards her covering. She is going to take hold of the aforementioned herself if the warmth and moisture are accurate and if all works well. Commonly, a serpent will drop once a period or indefinitely. Anticipate the tactic to urge the whole week. If there occur any difficulties, or worse-she might demand assistant if she hasn't discarded during a prolonged season.

A standard condition of shedding dilemmas may be a sterile atmosphere. Increase the moisture within the container, and supplement a crate somewhat full of moistened paper napkins, mildew, or other pliant bedding elements. This could be sufficient to answer the problem. A small little bit of moderate grazing beneath the mandible might likewise assist. Are there suitable things within the container for the serpent to brush on? She requires some flat stones and twigs for that. Subsequent all, she doesn't possess fingers. At this step, if your snake is yet not apt to form her discarding, bring her to the doctor, despite having worked the moistened paper napkins, boosting the moisture, and giving brushing areas.

5. Handling: Several pet serpents get to endure being touched; however, you want to not even venture to aim hand-training her until she has happily consumed a minimum of four feeds in her current place. Remain until there's no swelling from her feed before attempting to pet

her.

Begin gently and lay both palms beneath her abdomen to hold her mass. Solely touch the center portion of its frame, except if a doctor bids you're taking unless. There are several pharmaceutical purposes to stay her head or tailpiece, so if the doctor advises you to (for instance, for laundry the snake's front), move onward. In these situations, hold her frame together with your hand.

FUN FACTS

1. A general thin species.
2. The more inferior mandible is countersunk.
3. The eye is somewhat perpendicularly egg-shaped.
4. Sleek and glistening posterior coverings (not capitulated).
5. Coverings sprawl in 28-29 front lines, 27-31 midframe series, and 28-29 dorsal lines.
6. Exclusive anal plate.

THE END